RIVER OF WORDS

RIVER of

Murky Depths
Ryan Tremblay, age 17

WORDS

Images and Poetry

in Praise of Water

Edited by Pamela Michael
Introductory Essays by
Robert Hass and Thacher Hurd

Heyday Books • Berkeley, California

This project was supported by grants from The San Francisco
Foundation, from: an anonymous donor; the Susan and Arthur
Kern Fund; and the Jane Rogers and Michael Fischer Fund.

Library of Congress Cataloging-in-Publication Data

River of words : images and poetry in praise of water / edit-
ed by Pamela Michael ; introductions by Robert Hass and
Thacher Hurd.
     p. cm.
  ISBN 1-890771-65-1 (pbk. : alk. paper)
  1. Water--Poetry. 2. Children's writings, American. 3.
Youths' writings, American. 4. Children's writings. 5. Youths'
writings. 6.
Water in art. I. Michael, Pamela.
  PS595.W374R58 2003
  808.81'936--dc21
                                                    2003000729

Special acknowledgment is given to Amber Lotus, for provid-
ing several scans. The River of Words℠ Calendar is available
through their website at www.amberlotus.com.

Front Cover Art: *Quick as My Thought* by Rachel Rees
Back Cover Art: *Hidden River* by E. Jackson Darham
Cover and Interior Design: Rebecca LeGates

Orders, inquiries, and correspondence should be addressed to:
     Heyday Books
     P. O. Box 9145, Berkeley, CA 94709
     (510) 549-3564, Fax (510) 549-1889
     www.heydaybooks.com

Printed in China by Imago, Inc.

10 9 8 7 6 5 4 3 2

In memory of George A. Pughe, Jr., who loved children, believed in the value of education, and devoted his professional life to the people and programs of the Library of Congress, where River of Words was born

This printing made possible by the East Bay Municipal Utility District, recognizing 10 years of work by River of Words to inspire protection of local watersheds through literature and art

EBMUD

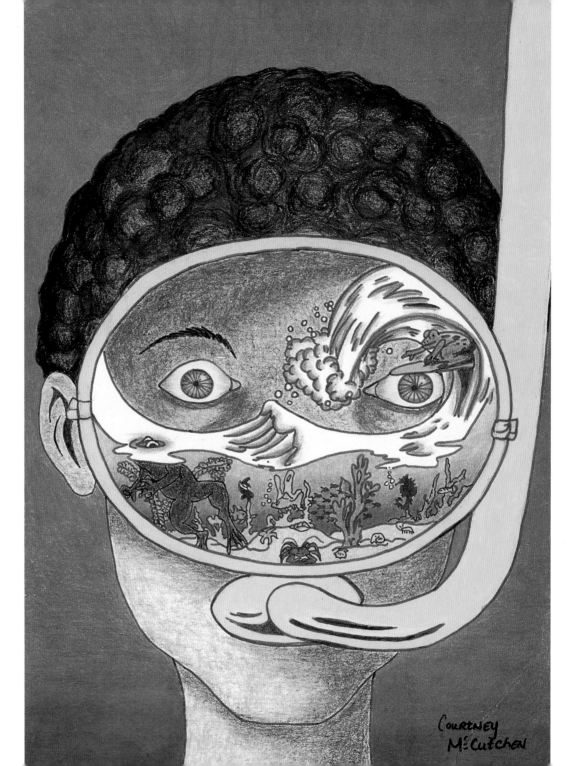

Submerge in
the Wonder

Courtney McCutcheon,
age 17

CONTENTS

Raging River

Ella Darham, age 8

THE LANGUAGE OF LANDSCAPE
Pamela Michael

*"There was a child went forth every day.
And the first object he looked upon, that
object he became. And that object became
part of him for the day or a certain part of
the day. Or for many years or stretching
cycles of years. The early lilacs became part
of this child. And grass and white and red
morning glories, and white and red clover,
and the song of the phoebe-bird."*
                                —Walt Whitman

At one time in the United States, not too
many generations ago, virtually everyone
grew up knowing what watershed they
lived in. Rivers then were our only inter-
state "highways"; most still ran wild across
the landscape and in the national psyche.
The central role they played in American
life was celebrated in story and song—
"Red River Valley," "Oh Shenandoah," *Life
on the Mississippi*. Children spent much of
their time outdoors, exploring the world
around them—searching knee-deep in
creeks for tadpoles, building forts in empty
lots, weaving daisy chains, collecting rocks,
climbing trees. Their experience of the nat-
ural world was visceral, frequent, and fun.
This investigative, hands-on approach to
learning is what River of Words® has spent

the last eight years re-introducing to the
educational process. One look at the art and
poetry in these pages—so full of energy and
place—affirms the wisdom (and astonishing
success) of our mission.

Nature has been the greatest source of
inspiration for artists and poets since
humans began drawing animals on the walls
of caves. Most of what we know of ancient
cultures has been gleaned from the artistic
expressions they left behind. Yet despite the
manifest importance of the arts and the
natural world they seek to interpret, the
state of both art and environmental educa-
tion in the United States reflects their mar-
ginalized status. Our forests and rivers are
tallied as resources, and the arts are consid-
ered peripheral at best, a self-indulgent fri-
volity. Decades have passed since botany,
geography, or natural history was paid more
than rudimentary attention in classrooms,
and only about half of our elementary
schools have full-time art teachers.

This devaluing of the very fundamentals
that sustain, define, and nurture us—our
land and our creativity—has already robbed
many of our children of a true sense of
belonging to a particular place. Few of
them have any real knowledge of where

their tap water comes from, where their garbage goes. They know little of who lived there before they did and what songs and stories they created, what art the landscape inspired. Few American schoolchildren can name more than a few of the plants or birds in their own neighborhoods, yet studies have shown the average American child can identify over one thousand corporate logos. This sorry scenario is increasingly true in other countries as well, even those with great regard for the role of art in society.

River of Words introduced its first "Watershed Explorer" curriculum in 1995. This place-based approach, teaching art and science in tandem, was hailed as innovative and particularly effective in getting students excited about learning. Our novel curriculum combined kite making and flying with the study of wind, atmosphere, birds, and aerodynamics. We coupled sketching and botany, nature journaling and poetry making, for instance, allowing children to explore topics creatively, using both left-brain and right-brain skills.

Because both art and science rely on observation and reflection, pattern recognition, experimentation, and critical thinking, we were surprised they weren't taught together more often. While revising and expanding our curriculum, however, poring over old textbooks for ideas, we realized our approach wasn't new after all: turn-of-the-century natural history texts were brimming with art, poetry, songs, and even a splash of spirituality. There was a sweet-

ness, a respect and love for nature and beauty in these earlier lessons that seemed worth emulating, especially in a world now so lacking in these qualities.

I remember finding my mother's childhood botanical sketchbooks in a trunk when I was eight or nine. They were a beautiful and complete rendering of the northern Illinois flora of her youth. I looked forward to the time in my own schooling when I would create a similar record of South Carolina's plants. That time never came: botany and plant identification somehow fell into a pedagogical crack in the 1950s, destined to become quaint, old-fashioned teaching relics, like the practice of memorizing poems. "Once upon a midnight dreary, while I pondered, weak and weary." Almost fifty years later, I still feel a gratifying sense of accomplishment when I recite that old chestnut. How many of today's children will have an opportunity to experience that same familiar comfort? How many will have the skills, knowledge, and imagination they will need to address the daunting environmental and social problems that twenty-first-century living most certainly will thrust upon them?

Bob Hass and I started a poetry and art contest for children on the theme of watersheds with the hope that focusing students' attention on their own homegrounds would give them an informed understanding of place that would help them grow into engaged citizens. We sought to nurture creativity and promote the idea that while not everyone can be an artist, everyone can be artistic. We've tried to add elements of wonder, discovery, interpretation, dexterity, and surprise to learning—natural history treasure hunts in schoolyards; oral history projects at senior centers; visits from local birders, farmers, or newspaper editors. Our small and hopeful idea has grown into a program that trains hundreds of teachers each year and touches the lives of tens of thousands of children annually. Hundreds of communities participate in River of Words—inspired art exhibitions, creek clean-ups, watershed festivals, poetry readings, award ceremonies, and celebrations. Can there be any doubt that education is the key to sustainable living, tolerance, and cross-cultural understanding?

"Beauty will save the world," Fyodor Dostoevsky said. We offer the thoughtful and heartfelt creations in this book from the children of the world as our best hope for the future.

About River of Words

River of Words® (ROW) trains teachers, park rangers, youth leaders, and other educators around the world on ways to incorporate nature and the arts into their own work with children. The organization was co-founded in 1995 by U.S. Poet Laureate (1995–1997) Robert Hass and writer Pamela Michael to promote literacy, watershed awareness, and the arts.

In affiliation with The Library of Congress Center for the Book (see Afterword), River of Words conducts an annual international poetry and art contest for children in kindergarten through twelfth grade on the theme of watersheds. ROW's "Watershed Explorer" curriculum, which combines history, math, science, social studies, geography, language, and the arts, helps children to develop an informed respect for the natural world as well as the skills and imagination they will need as engaged, active citizens.

River of Words publishes a book of winning entries to its art and poetry contest each year and also exhibits the children's work at museums, conferences, libraries, festivals, and other locations around the world.

For more information about River of Words, visit www.riverofwords.org.

Proceeds from the sale of this book will go toward continuing the work of this remarkable nonprofit organization.

ON WATERSHED EDUCATION
Robert Hass

If you put the earth's water—so I've read—into a gallon jug, just over a tablespoonful would be available for human use. Ninety-seven percent of the planet's water is in the ocean, and two percent is locked in icecaps and glaciers. A good deal of what's left lies in aquifers, often at inaccessible depths. But at any given moment in the earth's great hydrological cycle, about ninety thousand cubic kilometers of fresh water flow through rivers and lakes. It is this water, renewable but also contaminable and unpredictable and unevenly distributed, on which all earthly life depends. And it is this water we need to know how to preserve and share, if we are going to protect the quality of life on earth. That's why you're holding this book in your hands; our children, with their quick minds and sensuous aliveness, need to be educated to this task, and encouraging them to make art and poetry out of their experience of their own watersheds is one way to do this.

Water is everywhere, and everywhere it is local. In Yokohama Bay it is local to Yokohama, and in San Francisco Bay it is local to San Francisco. The survival of many Pacific life-forms depends upon the behavior of people who live beside those bays.

The Mississippi River is local when it flows through Minneapolis and local when it flows past St. Louis and local when it widens to a delta at New Orleans. Water is local in an Ecuadorian lake in the Andes where a flock of Baird's sandpipers, not yet an endangered species, is wintering; and it is local in the pond where they summer in northern Vermont, where local dairy farmers are in conversation with environmentalists about the once-clear water now burdened with algal blooms caused by the feces of the dairy cattle who produce the milk that produces the sharp cheddar cheese that someone in a café in New York is nibbling just now with a glass of wine made from grapes full of water that fell, locally, on a field in Bordeaux on a warm gray day five years ago.

Water is local and global and complicated because different distributions of water and weather in different geographies have made for different animal and plant species, and human beings symbolize themselves through the plants and animals they live among—in one landscape raven is trickster, in another coyote; people are tough as oak in European forests, tough as ironwood on African savannas. "Races of birds, subspecies of trees, and types of hats or raingear," as Gary Snyder has remarked, "often go by watershed": it is old knowledge that we make and are made by the places where we live.

And it is a new imperative—born of the many pressures on the planet and its biological life—that our children understand this. It is not something that the world we have created will necessarily teach them. The media that dominate our public life are always selling something: the news shows need to sell the news to deliver the audiences to the sellers of goods and services, and the other programs do the same, all at more or less the same feverish pitch. It's not exactly a public culture we intended, but it's the one that has come about. We have so far an only semi-articulated convention that we would not let this culture, which deluges our children in their daily lives, selling them mostly toys and sweetened foods, penetrate too deeply into our schools.

Meanwhile, many, many teachers are trying to figure out how to educate a new generation to the world they are going to inherit and how to do it in more useful and imaginative ways than most of us experienced. This is a movement that comes from the bottom up, from the life of the nation, its concerns and its ideals. Most of it is going on outside our schools of education and their certification programs, outside the public debate, such as it is, about the quality of our schools. Some of it is happening in the education programs of parks, in muse-ums of social and natural history, in alliances between departments of natural resources and local activists, and educators. Most of it is the work of dedicated and imaginative classroom teachers and of the environmentally concerned folk who work in local and national nonprofits. They have students in Pacific Northwest schools dancing the life cycles of salmon, and classrooms in Florida mapping the flow pattern of the Everglades. The poems and works of art by the children in this book come from classrooms all over the world, and they are part of the record of this upwelling.

If you think about the world's water supply, about access to clean water as a human right, about the enormous pressures of population growth and economic development, about the growing gap between rich and poor, about skeins of migrating birds flying toward their memory of feeding and nesting grounds, about the schools of fish in the bays where we load and unload our oil, about the difficulty of making even small changes in human behavior, and, thinking about these things, turn the pages of this book, seeing as the children see and understanding the concerns that have moved their teachers, you will feel the force of what these teachers are doing. A work of art, as the poet Adam Zagajewski observed, is a very small Noah's ark. But there is a flotilla of them here—and what pleasure there is in the words and images these children have made.

THE GIFT OF CHILDREN'S ART
Thacher Hurd

As someone who creates books for children, I am fascinated by children's art. It is filled with spontaneity, honesty, vital energy, and sometimes sheer beauty. Children haven't been taught the "right" way to use color and line. Their creativity bubbles up from within, without filters. Their distortions are full of life—a head is too large, but it feels right anyway because it is emotionally right. Hands, feet, gestures may look awkward, but they have an expressive quality that is missing in the art of adults. And the colors in children's art pour out in ways that defy rules.

When I first got a call from Pamela Michael asking me to judge the art for the River of Words contest, I didn't know what to expect. Judging a children's art contest? Deciding which child's drawing was the best? Classifying children's art? It seemed a difficult notion to put something so spontaneous into the narrow categories of a contest.

I had once entered a children's art contest myself, at the age of eight. I drew a picture of a turkey and sent it to the *San Francisco Chronicle*'s Junior Art Champion contest, a daily feature on the comics page in the fifties. Amazingly, my picture was a winner and my turkey was published on Thanksgiving Day in 1957. I was elated to see that what I had created on a piece of newsprint with a pencil and some poster paints could go out into the wider world. I still remember the feeling of excitement I felt: my picture had value to the larger world.

But now the thought of a children's art contest seemed daunting. Who was I to judge children's art, to come up with a grand-prize winner? I was dubious. A few weeks later I visited the River of Words office and Pamela began to show me the art they'd received from children of all ages, from all over the world. I was astonished by the variety before me: an enormous range of images, from as far away as Azerbaijan and as close as Berkeley. Some pictures were funny, some poignant, some deeply moving.

Looking at the art I realized that we react to children's art the same way we react to any art: it moves us from the heart. We judge it not on its technical polish (though some of ROW's artwork is beautifully rendered), but rather on our emotional reaction to it. Does it come alive? Does it touch us? Does its color dazzle? What does it have to teach us?

How do we evaluate it, though? We may use different criteria for judging children's art, but—make no mistake—it is as deeply connected to our inner world as any art, and perhaps more so than art created by adults, for children's art has fewer inhibitions and fewer intellectual pretensions.

As Pamela and I looked over the array of entries, I saw a much wider range of skills and sophistication than I had expected. Still, it seemed almost arbitrary to choose the "best." Then I realized that wasn't the point: the important thing was not who would win the prizes, but the fact that the contest and River of Words curriculum had sparked so many children to create art, to think about rivers and watersheds and wild places and their part in the life of our planet. The true "grand" prize is much greater than a trip to Washington, D.C., or a set of watercolors; the number of "winners" is greater by far than the number of entries to the contest. The great gift of River of Words is to nurture curiosity and artistic expression in young people, and to honor their creativity. The children's gift to us, in return, is their fresh and honest look at the world, one which gives us a rare, candid peek into the minds and hearts of those who will chart the future.

Rain Feeling

The nap time rain
sings lullabies
And throws all kinds
of flowers on your head
shimmering stars
and rainbows

Jessica Mozes, age 7

The Water's Task

Sometimes when it rains I feel small;
a comfortable small,
like a puzzle piece that fits just so.
The streets are always empty
as the drops parachute, roll and
unite in the gutter.
They are so sure in their task.
On these days I turn off the radio so
I can catch the glassy tick
of each drop on the roof.
Like tap shoes; like diamonds;
like tiny horses' hooves.
I imagine I am rooted in the soil,
my face lifted to receive the gift.
My roots like many ravenous hands
grasping the black dampness
of wet dirt.
I am always alone when the snails
flee their homes in droves.
I'm watching the ivy stretch upward
on the windowpanes and listening to
the symphony of drops.

Sarah Eggers, age 17

The River is the Basis of Life
Stanislav Shpanin, age 11

The Storm Is Coming

Wind whistles through
The pine needles twirl
Sawgrass sways
While clouds dash by

Little creatures hide
The pond waters splash
Rain gushes down
And tickles my toes

Kevin Brown, age 5

Watch, But Don't Touch
Aya Rothwell, age 16

The Rain

Dark
Pouring
Scary
Black
Puddle
Night

Maddison Boewe, age 6

What Happens After the Rain?

After the rain
water weaves its way through
silver strands
of the spider's web

Falling on berries
as red as a robin's belly

Making a dull red leaf
become a creamy brown

The sand,
which used to slip through my fingers
turns slimy and bumpy

The bark on an old willow tree
smells like a new penny

I feel a slight drizzle
left from the hard rain
falling down my back

This is what happens,
after the rain

Margie Lauter, age 10

The Night
Alex Schneble, age 7

Clean

The tires make a crushing sound
against the crust of the iced-over snow.

Frost webs are spun over the windshield.

Outside the sun reflects off the snow.
The white, bright light
makes me temporarily blind.

Finding salvation in the shadows,
I regain my sight.

I know that snow is pure.
But today, it is holy.

Forrest Carver, age 13

Untitled

A crystal
snowflake
falls down
on the
freezing
white
floor
of
January.

Martha Bregin, age 7

Canopy
Jennifer Mitchell, age 17

The Millionth Circle

Rippling outward
In
twinkling vibrations
Flickering under the silent
Orb of the moon
The stars giddy
With the sight of countless circles
The fish smile
A mere kiss can cause
a million circles

Leia Sandmann, age 12

Moon River
Kristina Fisher, age 17

I Am a River

I am liquid glass sparkling
pure and innocent,

I am the great ear of the world,
I hear the hurt, anguish, love and hate

I spy on romantic couples,
eavesdrop on father-son conversations

I hear murders being plotted,
see drugs being sold
I witness the slaughter of unarmed creatures

people ask me for advice, wishing,
hoping I have answers

I have heard a million things and am still astonished
by what people have the gall to think of
or worse,
even do.

Natalie Lasavanich, age 14

River in a Half Moon
Alima Aleskerova, age 14

15

Tenderness
of Cranes

Christian Jordan, age 8

The River's Music

Down from the rocky mountain
It gushes from a ledge.
A waterfall
Clear and tall
Cascading from the edge.

It rushes through a stream bed
Carved out by the work of time.
And fills a nook
With a bubbling brook
That adds to the water's rhyme.

It trickles through the forest
The vital veins of Earth.
And the woods resound
With the water's sound
And melodies of mirth.

Michelle Gruben, age 11

Untitled
Holly Heuer, age 11

18

River

of Life

flowing
carving its
way through
Tibetan   rocky
across wide   plateaus
Breaking the silence   nourishing   rolling plains
criss-crossing the   suds of country   rice fields
following soapy   through   washing
Zig-zagging   monuments   the Gorges
Impressive   the   guiding the
path of   developments   Yangtze
watching new   eyes opened   rise
smiling at   majestic   in awe
viewing the   thousand hidden   scenery
carrying a   depositing souvenirs   grains of memory
collecting,   growing   from its travels
in an ever   gold   treasure box
a pot of   of this   sparkling
at the end   rainbow   life giving

Ru-Woei Foong, age 11
This poem is in the shape of the Chinese character for water.

The River That Runs Through My Village

Michael Fulwiler, age 10

The River Flows
Narmina Ragimli, age 11

First Light

On that day, the first day, wise water,
heavy with our dreams
carries deep into the glen over rocks and through trees
until it reaches a dam.
And there standing on that dam shall be one man,
grown old and fat,
the man who betrayed the sun and moon.
He is standing, floating above the sick, dying river.
Behind him the water masses in a great rush.
Then, on that day the water will push
at the skeleton hands of cement until at last they
break before the water's wrath.
Then the water will rush free away from the man
and the broken remains of the dam.
The day shall rise with the sun and beauty will return to the land.
Water will flow again
and wonder will be seen glistening
as first light sparkles on the free water.

Graham Fischer-Corners, age 16

Don't Cut Off the Branch You're Sitting On

Valeriy Polushkin, age 12

Water Babies

La Llorona thrust her children
Into the river's mouth
And watched it swallow them
Like silver minnows.

Gleaming flies buzzed on the bus
Gasoline fumes floated, thin clouds over our heads
Juan and I shared an orange while *Abuelo* whispered,
In the USA we would eat ice cream every day.

Trudging through dense desert dusk,
We breathed the scent of green mesquite
Staring up at dark jagged mountains, down at tracks of tire sandals
Mama stumbled on a cattle guard.
Wrapped in her *rebozo*, the baby woke and whimpered.
Coyote Man whirled, hissing curses.

We reached the brown bubbling *mole* of the river
Our boats were plywood, laid over tubes
The Coyote snatched the child from her arms.
The weight of two would make it sink, he snarled.
Only a moment while he didn't watch
For the current to catch the fragile ship, carrying it away.

Mama didn't scream or speak at all
As they pulled her from the shallows.
Look, they cried, pointing to Juan and me
You have beautiful children still.
While her empty eyes sank into the swirling water
They led her away and the Coyote told my father,
I will not charge you for that child although the tube was lost.

La Llorona weeps for her children,
As they sink like stones.
Or do they float and twirl like trout
Living on mist and damselflies
In the circles of the river.

Todd Detter, age 17

Hidden River
E. Jackson Darham, age 11

Tears

If I cry for foolish things
Or
The troubles of the earth
I wonder
If my tears are the same
As the millions that were cried

In the Holocaust
The Famines
The Wars
The Murders
The Pollution

The Dying
The Jailings
The Drugs
The Shootings
The Slavery

All the troubles
Come with tears.
All the rivers
Flow with tears.
Cleansing tears.
Cleansing rivers.
Flow and heal.
Tears and rivers.
Flow and heal.
Water

Camila Perez, age 10

River Nymph
Leyla Guseynova, age 14

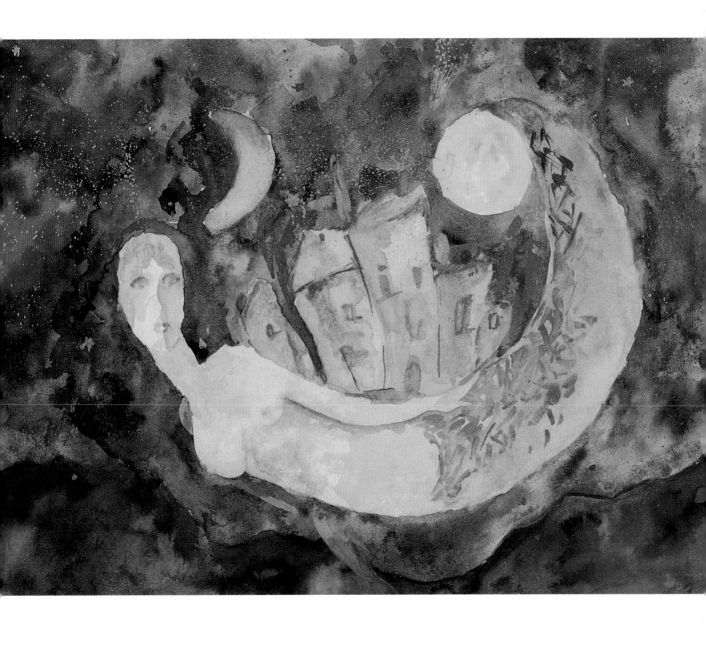

Our Dream

Chansereyeratna Lim, age 19

Just Imagine

Just imagine
Waking up one day,
Looking out your window
starting to say...

NO BAD SMELLS
NO SMOKE
NO NOISE
NO TRASH
NO CROWDED PLAYGROUNDS,
BASKETBALL COURTS,
OR CORNERS LOADED WITH TEENS.
NO BAD WORDS ON THE WALLS
AND SIDEWALKS
NO JUNK
NO MUDDY WATERS

NO HUNGER
NO POOR
NO PEER PRESSURE
NO ENVY
NO NAME CALLING

NO GUNS
NO FEAR

NO PAIN
NO MURDER
NO DRUGS

NO DEAD BIRDS BECAUSE OF
NO DEAD GRASS BECAUSE OF
NO DEAD TREES BECAUSE OF
NO DEAD PEOPLE BECAUSE OF
NO PLACE TO PLAY BECAUSE OF

CLEAN UP!
CARE!
HELP EACH OTHER!
PLAY!
GO OUTSIDE AND PLAY!
RUN!
SKIP!
JUMP!
RIDE!
SMILE!
BE HAPPY!
BE SAFE!
AND JUST IMAGINE BEING A KID
LIVING BY THE ANACOSTIA RIVER.

El'Jay Johnson, age 8

Coming Back to Skykomish

Cabin in the country
High on the hill
Overlooking the river

River rushes
Drops of compelling power
Keep on swimming, salmon

Proud mountain
Like a pointing finger
Snow melting in the sun

Forest awaits
Calling to the world
Trees two thousand strong

Sweet apple tree beckons
Gnarled branches outstretched
Calling, *Come Back*
         Come Back,
           This is the World.

Kate Lund, age 12

Loch Raven
Rachael Bakalyar, age 16

Rachael
Bakalyar

Dear Aquarius,

Tonight you bend
because the stars are fearless
enough to glow on you
They speak their truths in muted light
If one grain of sand is traced from a
twisting kiss in the North
to this forgiveness draped around my feet
then salvation lies in every loop and thrash
You keep your secrets well
in lengthy, passionate channels,
too gargling and gracefully
knitted to control
But Aquarius, I have
long held this view of you
basking in your semiprecious charm
When I was small, seven or so,
I'd put on brother's dingy jeans
and rill my way through silted grass,
to the steady saplings
blooming at your edge
Toe by toe, foot by dirtied foot
I disappeared
Everything from the mirror down
was me no more

Kt Harmon, age 17

The River of Life
Amy Williams, age 13

Reflections

Sometimes,
when the mountains
reflect on rivers,
you can find out things
you never knew before.
There are flowers up there,
rocks like clouds,
a little snow becomes a creek
and grows into a river.

Lindsay Ryder, age 11

Sunset in River
Khumar Gumbatova, age 13

Fishing

Cold this evening—
I'll blame the river.
Gazing on these stars
affords me some respite;
a cost-effective nepenthe.
Stuck between the act:
to
fish
or
to
bite?
It's rough when you're
the angler and the angled.
But, so it goes;
at once sedated, absorbed and secreted.
I am taken unawares
by this cricket,
whose chirping is cavernously
splendid tonight.

Mercury Ellis, age 17

The Catfish Are Jumping
Ryan Francis Rees, age 6

Dancing Catfish, the catfish are dancing

Fishing on the Ouachita

I burn my lure beneath the surface,
Cordell redfin, real as a rainbow
you like to feast on.

Starving striped bass
cruising for a bleeding shad,
you rise swift as white gulls above me,
deep from your blue hidden kingdom.

I wait for the moment
when I feel your strike
like a flood swallowing a levee.

Your fight breaks the water,
silver courage stronger than this line.
It gives, you take,
becoming my wish for another day.

Tyler Sellers, age 8

Trout Temptations
Stephen Rawl, age 14

Letter to the Architect

Not even you can keep me from
mentioning the fish, their beauty of
scaled brevity, their clipped-swishing
tails funneling in everything animal.
Wintertime when I saw them, their
pursed old ladies' mouths, gaping under
pooled clarity to share some gulled-up gossip.
Their bones, pure equilateral, poked stripes
at base and height, bereft of architects' errors
or human compensation. I remembered then
your last letter; you wrote you couldn't cut
another mitre, solder another joint, peel
another bit of glue from between your fingertips.
I'm going to crack soon, you said.
There must be some way to perfection
in this grasping for centimeters. The stick
will stay straight, the model be done,
done beautifully and done well someday.
I wrote back—I only know the cod with their
paling rib bones, their geometry unwarped by cold.
I know their tunnels dug frost-time underwater,
their crossings of snowflake symmetry. When
the thaws come, their finned bodies filter
the halfway ice like clean spectra.
You must know—the sight is exquisite.
If only I could give the gift of fish-making
in as many words as this.

Rebecca Givens, age 16

Quick as My Thought
Rachel Rees, age 10

Rachel

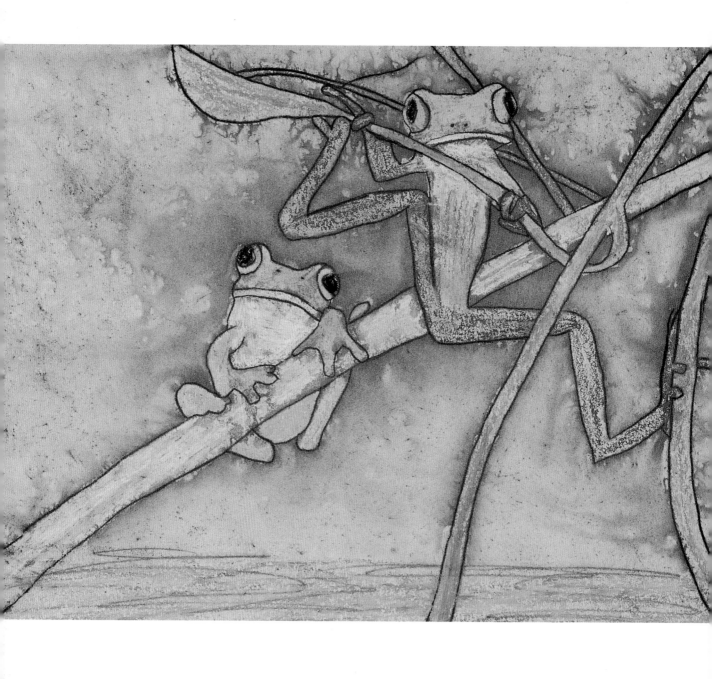

Davidson Creek

I was born in the
belly of that river.

again and again
    I go there

       to catch bullfrogs
       to lie flat on the wet
bank
          to let the brown snake
            slither past
       to find the meaning of life
          and lose it

to build my soul
    of rushes

       to paint your face
in the riverbed

       and go home
          dreaming of its
            voice.

Elizabeth Clark, age 17

Sisters
Toni Allen, age 12

The Evening Creek

Sit in the brush
with your straw hat on
and watch the creek.
Then get up and walk
on the banks, moonlit
with scattered touch-me-nots.
Walk closer to the creek,
and let the mud feel soft
on your bare feet.
Stop to look at jewel weed.
Hear the owl call.
Then dip your hand
into the pure water of the creek.
Walk home
with the taste of the sweet creek
in your mouth.

Suzi Alvarez, age 8

My Precious Water, I Kiss You

Parkpoom Poompana, age 15

Goldfish

Clear flowing
  Water
    Rushes down
      Stream
        As tiny
          Glazing
          Goldfish scatter
        To
        Their mother
    Like
Lightning.

Stefani Galik, age 8

Life at the River

Tarana Veliyeva, age 19

Water Shed Poem

Tread of pale stream,
Hemming watery licks.
And pebbles promise
Tootsie nooks
Burrowed scarce
Amongst the wind
And willow creep.
Finger tips,
Strain of sky,
Winged on ripping sun stripe.
Flight made on robin.
Torn in a scarlet
Slaughtered breast.
And moon bond leaves
Gilded in palms of dream brooks.

Lucy Barber, age 11

Watershed

Ilianna Salazar, age 8

Picture This

A babbling brook snaking its way through damp Seattle neighborhoods
And on its banks, vicious blackberries
Lurking behind every bend, ready to take the stream over,
like a pack of snarling wolves.

Imagine the maples
Each one giving their all to touch the sky.
One maple's adventure fails,
its last leaf flutters to the ground

A fork in the stream,
break off the trail and travel to another place, and time

Hear
The robin's call, mumble of water over the rocks

See the salmon
Every scale glistening in the morning sun

Stop here.

Luke Hussey, age 11

Salmon Spectacular

Cody Taylor, age 7

Johnny Pump Down

We siphon off water from
the Johnny pump.
Rebelliously and
Quite naturally.
For the simple
fact—
It's HOT!!!
No one
in their
right mind
gonna wait
to the
next rain drop.
Controllers
of the inner city,
Water irrigation systems—
Victims of
Water fights,
Get more,
but cops come around
Yellin 'bout they laws
We close up shop
till they leave
then enjoy summer once more.

David Reeves, age 17

The Children Play

Crystal Love, age 17

Amazon Slough Watershed

All summer long they come—
with or without dogs,
in loose, slow-moving bunches or
alone,
hiking the steep, narrow path past
the blackberries,
past the stream that is little more
than a trickle now
in the hot depths of summer.

In the winter the stream swells—
a vein, a pulsing artery of water
for deer that trip down from the
forest's edge,
for raccoons that hide by daylight
beneath our deck.
Chickadees, nuthatches, pine siskins
fly in and out of low brambly
willows that line the banks.

The stream dips beneath the surface,
through pipes, culverts, under streets

and out again, into the wan winter
sun
a quarter of a mile away where it
joins the slough,
brown floodwaters mingling.

Past ash and cottonwood,
in and out of cattails, willows,
past the place where each year
a family of ducks return
faithful to the stream,
and the huge blue heron is
sometimes seen.

Moving toward the river,
where geese honk overhead,
and finally to its end
in the marshy reservoir,
the tiny stream which began
across our street
has traveled eighteen long miles
and now mingles with other waters,
glistening in the sun.

Aaron Wells, age 12

Reflections
Alyson Duhon, age 13

Rockefeller Wildlife Preserve: Mid-August

The air is moist
The water bittersweet
A southern Gulf breeze sighs
Laughing gulls call
And cicadas click their
Luminous song
I smell the death scent
Of beached gars
And see the dreamy haze
Of oil on water
Nearby an alligator stares
With tabby eyes
A great heron startles
From its marsh bed
Standing on the rip-rap,
I peer at the water
And slowly hoist

The turkey neck on string
A blue-point crab
Grips the bait
I slyly dip the net
A good two feet away
And scoop up the crustacean
Without warning
And drop it into a bucket
To meet many friends,
Gifts of the Mississippi,
The day has reached its climax
Animals sleep through the heat,
Hiding in the wax myrtles
A snowy egret,
White plumage glistening,
Glides into the Roseau cane.

Kevin Maher, age 12

Sunbathing Flock

Christian Fernandes, age 10

61

Us Men

waterproofed to the waist,
see a vision, that to us
only comes once a year.
We are grumbling, stalking
out to the shed, to the purr
of engines warming.
Our breath spirits the chilled wind.
All day, work.
For the first time I am a part of it,
deserving of the reward that will come.
We sink back into cold metal bunkers
dug along gumbo levees
the color of potter's clay.
Dried stalks & weeds sway as cover.
In the distance, floodwater
rises against the sunburst ray
of a dying day. I hear the geese faintly
honk & gaggle above me. I see silhouettes
dot the horizon. There are splashes
of touch & go, wings flapping.
Yes, I do hope they like it here.
My father reaches for his boy,
                              and I give in.

Eric Wiesemann, age 15

Lazy Days

Elizabeth Sheridan Smith, age 17

The Heron

I want to paint its slender legs
As they move with grace
Slowly Oh so slowly
I want to dance its Arabian dance
moving with the water
Water rippling legs lifting
Slowly Oh so slowly
I want to fly like the heron flies
With an "Ark Ark,"
and a flutter of wings;
to fly away.
Swiftly very swiftly.

Leslie Blair Hewes, age 11

Heron

High
on 2 silver legs
blue ice cream
tipped wings
stretching
golden vanilla
beak,
creamy white neck
bent over shimmering water
silky smooth
peach fuzz wings
flooded
with a perfect
golden
ray of light
even stars
back away at its beauty.

Abigail Hemenway, age 10

Persephone Pondside
Kevin Maher, age 13

Invitation

Now I want only for you to dance with me.
Let's slip off our summer shoes, black with dust,
and stand in the froth, you—scared of this new
muddy rhythm, me—pulling you in.
You would budge, shifting off the bank, making us
four sun-blessed ankles in the cold water.
You'd have to listen to keep up with me,
to stay in time with the improvising shore.
Don't look mad as wavelets tease at the pant-leg
rolled thick over your knees.
Why not, instead, watch and hear the water
sing ungrammatically into the arms of the bay?
Notice it leads the willing fog,
open your hand and lean in.

But I know you, with your star-charts
and telescope. You mean to stand in the sky.

Dance with me anyway. Feel giddy
knees weaken. And while we grow planted
in the mud and your sun starts to dim,
melting into the water far away,
see your night sky tug at the darkening swells
until the heavens are liquid and Orion
breaks and its tadpole stars swim,
lighting the eyes of carp that brush our feet.
This is where things are whole, the nexus.
Dancing, sprouting fins and wings,
you would be knee-deep in the dream.

Valerie Madamba, age 17

Colorful Fishes in
the Beautiful River

Qanita Qamariani, age 7

Fish

Swimming in the river,
Curving her small shining body
Like shimmering stars swimming back
Into the deep sea
Being the fish of Joy.

Ella Schoefer-Wulf, age 9

What Are You Looking For?

Mamedov Rustam Gunduz, age 8

Ocean

Ocean
blue, gray, and green
gallops up to the shore
like a friendly puppy, licking
your toes.

Joanna Kass, age 11

Beavis
Thomas Bradley, age 13

AFTERWORD
John Y. Cole

DIRECTOR, THE CENTER FOR THE BOOK, THE LIBRARY OF CONGRESS

The Center for the Book in The Library of Congress is a proud River of Words® partner. Established in 1977 to use the resources and prestige of The Library of Congress to stimulate public interest in books, reading, and literacy, The Center for the Book has developed a national network of affiliated state centers and organizational partners that share its goals.

With its emphasis on encouraging creativity among young people and using words, art, and imagination to help youngsters connect with the world around them, River of Words is a natural Center for the Book partner, at both the national and state affiliate levels. There is another connection: River of Words co-founder Robert Hass was at The Library of Congress between 1995 and 1997 as Poet Laureate of the United States. The Center for the Book is pleased to continue its work with Mr. Hass through River of Words.

For seven years the annual awards ceremony for the River of Words student winners and finalists has been held at The Library of Congress. Sponsored by The Center for the Book, the program features poetry readings by the winning authors and a display of the winning works of art by their young creators. It is one of the Center's most popular public events. Proud parents and family members encourage the young poets and artists, making it a festive and meaningful occasion. The community and educational outreach aspects of the project are highlighted. Above all, however, the spirit of River of Words—a project that brings out the best in all of its participants—shines through. That spirit also is most evident in the book you have before you.

Wild and Free—the River and Me

Naomi Celmo, age 15

CONTRIBUTORS

Alima Aleskerova *River in a Half Moon,* (The Palace of Children & Youth Creative Work, Baku, Azerbaijan. Teacher: Tatyana Kesar), p. 14

Toni Allen *Sisters,* (Broadmoor Middle Magnet School, Baton Rouge, LA. Teacher: Alan Morton), p 46

Suzi Alvarez "The Evening Creek," (Abington Friends School, Elkins Park, PA. Teacher: Jane McVeigh Schultz), p. 48

Rachael Bakalyar *Loch Raven,* (Good Shepherd School, Baltimore, MD. Teacher: Ariadne Gejevski), p. 35

Lucy Barber "Water Shed Poem," (Denver School of the Arts, Denver, CO. Teacher: Jana Clark), p. 52

Maddison Boewe "The Rain," (Pine Knob Elementary School, Clarkston, MI. Teacher: Beth Gifford), p. 6

Thomas Bradley *Beavis,* (University School at University of Tulsa, Tulsa, OK. Teacher: Tim Bradley), p. 70

Martha Bregin "Untitled," (Pine Knob Elementary School, Clarkston, MI. Teacher: Paula Boehman), p. 10

Kevin Brown "The Storm Is Coming," (Lake Park Baptist School, Lake Park, FL. Teacher: Mrs. Long), p. 5

Forrest Carver "Clean," (Center for Teaching and Learning, Edgecomb, ME. Teacher: Nancie Atwell), p. 10

Naomi Celmo *Wild and Free—the River and Me,* (Fort Myers High School, Fort Myers, FL. Teacher: Irene Linn), p. 74

Elizabeth Clark "Davidson Creek," (Chase County High School, Imperial, NE. Teacher: Shelly Clark), p. 47

E. Jackson Darham *Hidden River,* (Home-schooled, Bozeman, MT. Teacher: Nan Darham), p. 28

Ella Darham *Raging River,* (Home-schooled, Bozeman, MT. Teacher: Nan Darham), p. x

Lauren De Mers *Yellow Salamander,* (Richmond Elementary School, Susanville, CA. Teacher: Petra Rees), p. 78

Todd Detter "Water Babies," (North High School, Phoenix, AZ. Teacher: Mrs. Buehler), p. 26

Alyson Duhon *Reflections,* (L.J. Alleman Middle School, Lafayette, LA. Teachers: Lana Badeaux and Debra Blair), p. 58

Sarah Eggers "The Water's Task," (Point Loma High School, San Diego, CA. Teacher: C. Hedges), p. 2

Mercury Ellis "Fishing," (School of the Arts, San Francisco, CA. Teacher: Gene Mattingly), p. 40

Christian Fernandes *Sunbathing Flock,* (Durban Avenue School, Hopatcong, NJ. Teachers: Mrs. Wentink and Mrs. McManus), p. 60

Graham Fischer-Corners "First Light," (Denver School of the Arts, Denver, CO. Teacher: Jana Clark), p. 25

Kristina Fisher *Moon River,* (Santa Fe Preparatory School, Sante Fe, NM. Teacher: Geoff Stewart), p. 12

Ru-Woei Foong "River of Life," (Shanghai American School, Shanghai, China. Teachers: Brian Compton and Angela Kocher), p. 20

Michael Fulwiler *The River That Runs Through My Village,* (International Community School of Abidjan, Abidjan, Ivory Coast. Teacher: Octavia McBride-Ahebee), p. 21

Yellow
Salamander

Lauren De Mers,
age 14